BOOK INDEXING

M. D. ANDERSON

The right of the University of Cambridge to print and sell all manner of books was granted by Henry VIII in 1534. The University has printed and published continuously since 1584.

CAMBRIDGE UNIVERSITY PRESS

CAMBRIDGE

NEW YORK   NEW ROCHELLE

MELBOURNE   SYDNEY

Published by the Press Syndicate of the University of Cambridge
The Pitt Building, Trumpington Street, Cambridge CB2 1RP
40 West 20th Street, New York, NY 10011-4211, USA
10 Stamford Road, Oakleigh, Victoria 3166, Australia

First published 1971
Reprinted with corrections 1979
Revised and reprinted 1985
Reprinted 1987, 1991

Printed in Great Britain by Athenaeum Press Ltd, Newcastle upon Tyne

ISBN 0 521 08202 1

IN PIAM MEMORIAM

G.V. CAREY

CONTENTS

BOOK INDEXING

QUALIFICATIONS OF AN INDEXER

'The true aim of an indexer', wrote G. V. Carey, in *Making an Index* (Cambridge University Press, 1951), 'is to be methodical rather than mechanical, and the best indexer is he who is most generously endowed with common sense.'

The indexer should also have a bent for sorting and classifying, without which the laborious side of indexing outweighs the satisfactions. A good fund of miscellaneous information is helpful, and the indexer should understand the matter he is to index. Books for the general reader on most subjects may be tackled by the 'general indexer', but some specialist works, especially legal and scientific, have their own languages, which the indexer must know. The remaining qualifications of an indexer come with practice. It is difficult to teach indexing; there are few hard-and-fast rules, and much that can only be learnt by experience. To show how to set about gaining skill, with notes on likely pitfalls, is the object of this guide.

EQUIPMENT I

There are other methods. For small indexes, a thumb-indexed notebook or bunch of paper may be used. A few people, in this resembling such early indexers as H. B. Wheatley, like to write the successive entries one under the other on sheets of paper, or type them on perforated rolls, and then separate them and arrange them in alphabetical order for final typing. The entries are thus kept at first in order of occurrence, which has some advantages. But with a book of any length, and entries of any complexity, separate cards are essential. It pays to sort them into alphabetical order as soon as it becomes difficult to retrieve a card from an unsorted handful.

Cards are most easily handled when of firm but flexible

texture, i.e. thin cards rather than thick paper. Cardboard boxes, such as shoe-boxes, make convenient containers for indexers working at home, being light to carry and store. The more professional card-index drawers are scarcely more convenient. It is usual (but not necessary) to sub-divide the cards by guide-cards with letters of the alphabet, or smaller sections if necessary.

Most indexers like to work at a table or desk with space to lay out cards. But it is rarely necessary to lay out more than four or five cards at a time, so that a writing-board on the knees by the fireside may be preferred by those working at home. More space may be needed if the current cards are kept out of the box during a spell of work, say on one chapter of a book, which is a good plan if each chapter deals with a well-defined section of a subject, but has fewer advantages for books of diffuse structure. The question of lay-out space does not arise for indexers working on the system of writing successive entries on sheets of paper, for they make a fresh entry every time the same name or topic appears, and do not have to seek an existing card. But they do need space later, when they have to cut up their sheets of paper and sort their entries.

Besides cards and boxes to hold them, an indexer working on someone else's book is liable to need reference books. Dictionary, biographical dictionary, and atlas or gazetteer are the basic requirements; others readily suggest themselves. For solving problems relating to, say, the new African countries, or to recent scientific developments, up-to-date books are necessary, and difficulties of replacement may make it necessary to consult these in libraries. But anyone intending to do much indexing should miss no chance of acquiring useful reference books, secondhand if necessary, and they should stand at his elbow.

EQUIPMENT II: COMPUTERS

Some readers may ask: why use index cards at all? Why not put the index entries straight into a computer?

The computer-assisted index has certainly come to stay, and

2

indexers must consider whether they would profit by investing in a home computer, or employing a computer-service firm, or whether they should continue with 'manual' indexing only.

The procedure for a computer-assisted index is somewhat as follows. The indexer marks on the proofs the words that are to become headings and sub-headings in the index. These are typed into the computer, which is programmed to arrange them in alphabetical order, with sub-headings appropriately placed. From the computer disc (or tape), a printout is obtained.

Provided that a well-constructed program is used and that the computer operator understands indexing, the result may be an adequate index for a book in which names of people, places, or things form the bulk of the indexable material. Such indexes are, of course, those that are most easily and quickly compiled 'by hand', and the fee charged by a computer-service firm for a printout from a marked set of proofs is apt to be of the same order as that paid by the publisher for the index. It would be interesting to have a study of the comparative costs of indexing with a home computer.

As the topics of the text become more complex and theoretical, the more the resources of the program are strained, and the more the indexing experience needed by the operator. At some level of difficulty of text, depending on the capabilities of program and operator, the revision and reorganization of the longer index entries becomes so extensive that better results are obtained by working with cards, than with the computer. For really good indexes to important books, 'manual' indexing is indispensable. In the words of the *Chicago Manual of Style*, 'Indexing requires decision-making of a far higher order than computers are yet capable of.'

The advantages claimed for the computer are that it relieves the indexer of drudgery, and that it saves time. The drudgery usually mentioned is the process of alphabetization. But the 'manual' indexer does not find this laborious, for it is done imperceptibly as new cards are added, a few at a time, to those already in order. Typing the index entries into the computer probably takes about the same amount of time as writing them on cards. So far any saving of time is unimportant. The real saving of time and work is in the printout, which eliminates the stage of typing the index from the cards. And there is a further, and very important saving, in that the computer disc can be directly used for computer typesetting, thus cutting out a whole stage in book production.

A field in which computers can be particularly useful is in the preparation of indexes for very long texts of basically simple nature, that are either published annually, or go into new editions at short intervals, as with some medical and law textbooks. If alterations and additions are not too extensive, the computer disc can be updated for the new issue, and used again for typesetting.

It may be added that though the following pages refer to 'manual' indexing, the processes there described for planning the index, and selecting and arranging the entries for it, are the same for computer-assisted as for any other indexes.

PLANNING THE INDEX

I. GETTING ACQUAINTED WITH THE BOOK

Though it is possible to index from galley proofs (see p. 27), or even from MSS, a book is most easily indexed when it is in page proof, and usually there is not then much time available before the index copy is required. Sometimes the proofs reach the indexer in batches, and only a few days may separate the arrival of the last batch from the date on which the completed index must be ready. The proofs may arrive later than scheduled, whereas the date on which the index is wanted is apt to be rather inflexibly fixed. These are facts of life for indexers. But whatever the need for haste, it is imperative to give some thought to planning the index before starting to work on it.

The index must be appropriate for the book. What kind of book is it? The best way of finding out is of course to read it, but in practice there is rarely time to read it through, even if all the proofs are available. It is a help to study the list of contents carefully, but this important part of the book is often the last to reach the indexer. The author has a great advantage over any other indexer in knowledge of the book, hence the saying that whoever writes the book, the author should index it. But all authors have not the time for indexing, nor necessarily the aptitude. Some author-made indexes have earned the Wheatley Medal, the only honour awarded for indexing; others are examples of how not to do it. Furthermore, some books have several authors. So there are bound to be non-author indexers, and they have to do their best, often under difficulties, to become acquainted with their texts.

2. TYPE OF INDEX

Given some knowledge of the scope of the book and the treatment of the subject, experience indicates the type of index required. For those lacking experience, a detailed study of indexes to books on similar subjects is a good foundation on which to build. The range of possible indexes runs from the 'light' biography or book of travel, needing only an alphabetical list of names of people and places, to the multi-volume scientific textbook, which must be indexed in great detail to make its contents readily available.

The basic function of indexing is analytic, breaking down the contents of a book into small sub-divisions, and re-arranging them alphabetically. But some indexers conclude the analytic process by new syntheses, gathering together all examples of one type of subject. For example, a synthetic indexer of a book on history might assemble all treaties between nations under 'treaty', while the analytic indexer would leave them as:

> Amiens, Treaty of (1802)...
> Utrecht, Treaty of (1713)...
> Versailles, Treaty of (1919)...
> Westphalia, Treaty of (1648)...
>   etc.

A synthetic indexer might construct a long entry for trade:

> trade: in grain...; in oilseeds...;
>   in spices...; in timber; etc.

The analytic indexer would leave these entries as:

> grain, trade in...
> oilseeds, trade in...
>   etc.

The synthetic indexer may be expected to supply cross-references:

> grain, trade in, *see under* trade
> oilseeds, trade in, *see under* trade
>> etc.

The analytic indexer may have

> trade, *see under individual commodities*

or 'trade', with a few page references to general accounts of trade, followed by: *see also under individual commodities*.

A fine example of the synthetic method is Mrs Quinn's Wheatley-Medal index to the facsimile reprint of Hakluyt's *Principall Navigations* (Cambridge University Press, 1965), in which, for example, she collects all the articles of Elizabethan trade in an entry for commodities, to which there are cross-references from the various items. Such syntheses may be most thought-provoking, and provide indexes that can be read for their own sake. A synthesis required by some authors is the collection of all Acts of Parliament under that heading, instead of under Education Act, National Insurance Act, etc. Some syntheses are merely tiresome, as in those cookery books that have a few enormously long index entries for Soups, Sauces, Fish dishes, Meat dishes, Puddings, and Cakes, and hardly any other entries at all.

Analytic indexes are characteristic of most specialist scientific textbooks. People do not read these books from cover to cover; they refer to them for information on some particular point, and are likely to be seeking some highly specific word – not amines, or aromatic amines, or naphthylamines, but 1,5-diaminonaphthylamine. They do not expect individual substances or species collected under the group to which they belong. On the other hand, indexes of scientific books meant for students rather than specialists may sometimes advantageously have a certain number of synthetic entries, which assemble examples of some process or reaction.

Some indexes may be called informative. They give dates of birth and death and a few descriptive words for individuals, or dates of beginning and end of reign for monarchs. County or country is added to place-names, and explanations are given for unusual terms. Such indexes are valuable adjuncts to school-books.

3. LENGTH OF INDEX

After type of index, length of index may have to be considered. Sometimes length is left to the indexer's judgment – a happy state of affairs for him, unless doubts arise in his mind as to whether he is under-indexing or over-indexing. The index may then be usefully compared in length with those of similar books. The length of an index relative to the length of the book is sometimes given merely as the number of pages of index expressed as a percentage of the number of pages of text. But it is better to calculate in lines, for an index is almost always printed in smaller type than the text, and the number of lines on a page of index varies from as little as 10 % to as much as 120 % above the number on a page of text. The number of lines from top to bottom of a page of index, multiplied by the number of pages in the index, and expressed as a percentage of the approximate number of lines in the rest of the book, gives a rough estimate of the relative length of the index. For a more accurate estimate, lay-out of the index would have to be taken into account. Also, those rare indexes with only one column would have to be rated lower, and those with three or four columns higher, than the usual two-column index.

Using this method of reckoning, it is found that short indexes run from 1 % to 3 % of the text, indexes for many 'serious' books for the general reader from 4 % to 7 or 8 %, and those for specialized textbooks up to 15 %.

Sometimes the publisher fixes the length, and allots the indexer so many two-column pages, with so many lines to the column, and so many characters per line. To meet these requirements, first find out whether the space allows for a short or a long index. Suppose that the book has 300 pages, with 40 lines per page; that is 12,000 lines. Suppose also that there is to be a 12-page index, with 50 lines per page; that is 600 lines – in practice a few less, to allow for the heading, and spaces between the letters of the alphabet; 600 is 5 % of 12,000, so the index can be of medium length. The 600 lines in double column would allow for 1,200 entries if none were longer than the width of the column. But a considerable fraction will run over on to another line, so that 1,000 entries at most should be aimed at. This will almost certainly be too many, but the index can be adjusted to the space by a final judicious pruning. And distressing as it is for the indexer to have to cast overboard some of his entries, the index may turn out to be better without them. An estimate of progress can be made by counting (in lines) the entries made for, say, one-quarter of the book, and the indexer can then alter his coverage if necessary. It might appear that only about three references per page of text could be afforded for the book imagined above, but this is not so, for the same name or subject will in many cases have several page references following it; 1,000 entries means 2,000 or 3,000 or even more page references.

If many indexes have to be made to specified length, it saves time to measure the thickness of, say, 200 cards tightly pressed together; the resulting figure is quite accurate enough for rough calculations, if combined with a quick estimate of the number of entries taking more than one line.

4. LAY-OUT OF INDEX

A factor in the length of an index is the arrangement of the sub-headings. They may be 'run on' (1) or 'set out' (2):

(1) Cambridge, 1–2, 5–10; colleges in,
　　12–25, 29, 34–5; industries in, 26–30;
　　population of, 11, 12; river at, 3, 4

(2) Cambridge, 1–2, 5–10
　　colleges in, 12–25, 29, 34–5
　　industries in, 26–30
　　population of, 11, 12
　　river at, 3, 4

The choice between the methods may be dictated by the publisher, or by exigencies of space, for obviously run-on sub-headings take fewer lines. If the choice is left to the indexer, he need not make a decision until the typing stage, but he must remember that run-on sub-headings do not accommodate sub-

8

sub-headings comfortably, though it is possible to introduce a limited number by the use of brackets:

> Cambridge, 1–2, 5–10; colleges in, 12–23,
>   34–5, (women at) 24–5, 29; industries
>   in, 26–30; population of, 11, (including
>   undergraduates) 12; river at, 3, 4

With set-out sub-headings and run-on sub-sub-headings, this would be:

> Cambridge, 1–2, 5–10
>   colleges in, 12–23, 34–5; women at
>   24–5, 29
>   industries in, 26–30
>   population of, 11; including
>   undergraduates, 12
>   river at, 3, 4

Or, with both sub-headings and sub-sub-headings set out in the spacious style of older indexes:

> Cambridge, 1–2, 5–10
>   colleges in, 12–23, 34–5
>   women at 24–5, 29
>   industries in, 26–30
>   population of, 11
>   including undergraduates, 12
>   river at, 3, 4

A possible compromise is to have most of the entries with run-on sub-headings, but to set out those for a few especially complex ones.

Sometimes an entry that has too many sub-sub-headings for comfort in the run-on style can be brought to order by dividing it into several entries. A good example is the compound ribonucleic acid, or RNA. In a book on biochemistry, RNA may often appear in that form, but also in the forms of messenger or mRNA, ribosome or rRNA, and transfer or tRNA. To force all these into one entry may be a hopeless task if the sub-headings have to be run on, but division into four successive entries can solve the problem:

> RNA...
> mRNA...
> rRNA...
> tRNA...

and they can then each have a series of sub-headings of their own. Even with set-out sub-headings, it simplifies matters to have the separate entries.

The sub-headings for the entry for Cambridge above were arranged alphabetically. Opinions differ as to whether alphabetically in this connection should mean alphabetically by first significant word (1), or alphabetically taking prepositions, etc., into account (2):

(1) law	(2) law
codification of	codification of
of colonies	in travel communities
on duelling	of colonies
of mining camps	of mining camps
in travel communities	of vigilantes
of vigilantes	on duelling

Method (1) is more usual with word-by-word indexing, method (2) with letter-by-letter indexing (see below).

Sometimes sub-headings are ranged chronologically instead of alphabetically, especially in biographies and books on history, in which chronological order often agrees fairly closely with order of appearance in the book. Or the sub-headings may be put in numerical order of the first page reference after each.

Many indexers would write the entry for Cambridge as follows:

Cambridge
colleges...
industries...
population...
river...

with no relating prepositions. This form is compact, and easily intelligible in this example, in which the sub-headings all stand in much the same relation to the key word. In more complex entries, the fuller form has advantages of style as well as of clarity.

5. METHOD OF ALPHABETIZATION

There are two ways of arranging index entries alphabetically, and an early choice between them will save time and possible confusion later on. Most readers will not notice which method has been used, adapting themselves unconsciously to what they find, but if the indexer has mixed the two methods, readers may miss an entry, and will have a legitimate cause for complaint.

When using the so-called word-by-word ordering, each word of compound headings (consisting of more than one word) is alphabetized separately. Thus, in the left-hand column below, all expressions beginning with 'red' standing alone are ranged in order before any in which 'red-' is part of a word. In the other, or letter-by-letter method (right-hand column), the same expressions are alphabetized as if they were each a single word:

Red Cross	Redcar
Red Ensign	Red Cross
Red Indians	Redemptorists
Red Sea	Red Ensign
Redcar	Redesdale, Lord
Redemptorists	Red Indians
Redesdale, Lord	Redmond, John
Redmond, John	Red Sea

The difference between the methods is particularly noticeable for entries consisting of initials (except where the initials have lost their full stops and become acronyms, which are treated as words). Thus in the word-by-word ordering, B.B.C. is treated as if B was a word on its own, and is placed at the head of the entries for B, whereas in the other method it comes after all words beginning Ba:

B.B.C.	bagpipes
bagpipes	Bath
Bath	B.B.C.
beacons	beacons

In the examples above, the alternative places of a given word are not very distant from each other, and it would no doubt be found by the index-user. But in really long pieces of alphabetization, change of method may shift a word by 100 places or several columns, so that it is not an unimportant matter.

Word-by-word ordering is commonly used for unspecialized books; it is also found in Roget's *Thesaurus*. Letter-by-letter ordering is used in encyclopaedias and atlases, and in *Whitaker's Almanack* and has advantages for technical books, especially in the fields of chemistry and engineering, in which there are many compound expressions that may on occasion be written as two words, as hyphenated words, or as one word.

In word-by-word ordering, hyphenated words should be treated as one word if either part cannot stand alone (Pre-Raphaelite, anti-Semitism), otherwise as two words (half-holiday, card-index).

Unhyphenated compound names should be indexed according to usage:

Lloyd George, David
Vaughan Williams, Ralph

Alphabetization by either method is carried as far as the first comma or other mark of punctuation, and then renewed:

National Defence, Council of
National Defence Act
National Gallery, London
National Gallery of British Art, *see* Tate Gallery
National Insurance, *see under* Social Security
National Insurance Act
National Museum, Washington
National Museum of Antiquities of Scotland

The usage with regard to significant and minor words is liable to vary between the two methods of alphabetization. In word-by-word ordering, only significant words are usually considered, but in the letter-by-letter system the prepositions, etc., are commonly taken into account. Thus the index to the *Encyclopaedia Britannica* (14th edition) has:

National Society for the Promotion of Industrial Education
National Society of Day Nurseries

A word-by-word indexer would probably reverse the order.

Chemical prefixes, such as m, r, and t in front of RNA (see p. 9), and also α-, β-, and γ-, o-, m-, and p-, N-, S-, and figures, are all ignored in alphabetization, except, of course, that m-benzoquinone precedes o-benzoquinone. Formerly the words were aligned and the prefixes printed to the left of the column, but it is now more usual for the prefixes, though ignored alphabetically, to be treated as part of the word in aligning. *Cis-*, *trans-*, and cyclo-, which used to be counted as prefixes, now tend to become part of the word, in both alphabetization and aligning.

6. ONE OR MORE INDEXES

Another matter that must be settled at the outset is whether to have one or more indexes. Here again the publisher may give directions. On the whole, index-users appreciate a single comprehensive index, but there are exceptions. Lawyers are accustomed to a separate index of law cases cited, and scientific books that refer to numerous original papers are usually provided with a separate index of authors. Biological works mainly concerned with taxonomy sometimes have an index of species mentioned. Theological books may have an index of Biblical quotations, and books on classical authors an *index locorum* of references to the texts under discussion. But to give several indexes to a non-specialized book, perhaps of people, places, books, and general topics, as is sometimes done, is an unnecessary complication.

When two indexes are wanted, say of authors and subjects, they are best carried out as distinct pieces of work, for different skills seem to be involved in the mechanical collection of numerous authors' names, and in the dissection of the meaning of the text to find suitable index entries, and trying to do both at once is irksome and difficult. Though two complete traverses of the book must be made, they can be run intercurrently; a spell of work on one index, followed by a spell on the other, gives pleasant variety – which is fortunate, because if the proofs are arriving in batches, the alternation may be unavoidable.

Note that author indexes should not include references to units, apparatus, processes, or equations called by authors' names. Amperes, coulombs, and newtons, Geiger counters and Nicol prisms, Lorentz invariance and Zeeman effect, should be entered in the subject index.

MAKING THE INDEX: I

1. CHOICE OF ENTRIES

Planning the index is not such a lengthy affair as the foregoing pages may have made it seem. Once a preliminary routine has been established, the various decisions for a given index are soon made, and the actual work of compiling it can begin.

Choosing the entries from the text exercises all the powers of the indexer, who must be alert not only to the words of the author, but also to the meanings behind them, and to the inter-relations of different parts of the book. The attention must move to and fro between large-scale subjects of whole chapters, and small details of description, and each must be assessed with regard to the likely needs of the index-user. In this exercise of choice and assessment lies the difference between a mechanical indexing of words, which can now be done by a computer, and that perception and appreciation of the author's ideas, and their arrangement in the form most helpful to the reader, which makes a good index into a work of art.

The coverage for a particular book often has to be a compromise between what the indexer would like to include, and what the available space will take. Coverage must not be erratic; however lightly or densely a book is indexed, the aim should be to have about the same proportion of index to text throughout, of course allowing for different degrees of what might be called indexability and index-worthiness in different parts of the book. Uneven coverage can occur when the indexer finds some sections of the book more interesting than others. Novice indexers often start by heavily over-indexing, but in spite of this, 'when in doubt include' is a good rule, for superfluous entries can (indeed must) be discarded later on, but it may be difficult to recover some name or topic passed over many pages earlier, and now found to be important. This of course does not mean that the index should be choked with trivialities; always ask yourself who is going to use the index, and for what purpose; in fact, is your entry really necessary?

2. PREFACE

The preface of a book rarely needs indexing, but should not be ignored. The names of people to whom the author expresses his thanks need not be indexed, but there may be a mention of some other author whose work is being confirmed, extended or controverted in the book. A decision is needed as to whether the index is to contain entries for these modern writers on the author's subject. If the names are assembled in a bibliography, they need not be included in the index also. But if there is no bibliography, and mentions are not too numerous and give useful information, then index entries for them are probably wanted. When there are large numbers of such names, author or publisher should be consulted about indexing them. Names that are included in the bibliography may of course occur in the text in other connections than as authors of the books quoted, and should then be considered for indexing in the usual way.

3. INTRODUCTION

The introduction or introductory chapter, unlike the preface, is part of the book, and must be treated in the same way as the rest, with the proviso that sometimes it is easier to understand and index the introduction last, instead of first. It may assume a familiarity with the subject which the indexer will acquire while working on the book, but may not possess at the outset.

4. CHAPTER HEADINGS

Next consider the heading of the first chapter; does it suggest an index entry? It may be an obliquely descriptive epithet, resembling the title of a novel, when it can be passed by. Or it may be used in a rather vague way, and be found to refer to part only of the following pages, when the title can be indexed with that particular part as the reference. But often it describes the contents of the chapter accurately, and is indexable in form and meaning, and the reader can rightly expect to find it in the index. Yet it is not unusual for chapter headings to be ignored by the indexer, who fails to inform the reader that there is a whole chapter about a given subject.

The question of insertion of chapter headings in the index brings up another matter of policy. If a chapter is not long, and contains practically all that is said on the subject in the book, an entry might run as follows:

France, 21, 52, 67–83, 110

where 67–83 is easily seen to refer to the chapter with the main account. A convention is sometimes established of emphasizing these figures by bold type, or by placing them first in the string of page numbers.

But suppose that the book is a large history of Europe, with chapter 5 headed France, and many references to France scattered through other chapters. The entry for France will need careful consideration; is it to be one long, much subdivided entry, or should the sub-divisions have entries in their own right? If one long entry is chosen, it may be thought unnecessary to include 'France, 67–120' for chapter 5, since the contents should be covered in the sub-headings. But if French kings, wars, naval battles, economic conditions, politics, relations with other countries, literature, etc., are found under separate headings, then the general references under 'France' should include 'France, 67–120' for chapter 5.

A faulty formula sometimes found is of the type:

France, 67–120
    army of, 45–7, 164, 172
    literature of, 183, 309–16
    social conditions in, 220–4

where the page references for the sub-headings are all from chapters other than chapter 5, and mentions of the topics of the sub-headings within chapter 5 are ignored. Here indexing the chapter heading leads to a misrepresentation.

5. SUB-DIVISIONS OF CHAPTERS

After the chapter heading, any sub-divisions of the chapter may be considered for indexing, before attending to the actual text. This quick preview of the chapter serves to show what are the main topics, and what details are likely to be important.

6. FOOTNOTES AND ENDNOTES

The indexer should not overlook the notes; they contain not only the names of other writers on the subject of the book, a matter dealt with above, but also occasional indexable items of information. A page reference to a footnote should be distinguished as 112n, unless the matter is also referred to in the text above, when page number alone is enough. It may be helpful to put 112 n. 5, if the footnotes are unusually numerous. A reference to an endnote requires the note number and the page on which the note appears.

MAKING THE INDEX: II

I. PROPER NAMES

The most obvious candidates for inclusion in the index are proper names, and picking out the words beginning with capitals is the basis of many simple indexes. But the mention of a name must be meaningful if it is to be indexed. In such expressions as:

> Before the time of Julius Caesar...
> After the death of Nelson...
> In towns other than London...
> West of the Mississippi...

the names are used as reference points, not for their own sakes, and they should not be indexed. One can of course imagine superficially similar phrases that probably would need entries for the names, because they are followed by items of information:

> Before this time, Julius Caesar had...
> Nelson's death was the subject of...
> London, alone of towns...
> The Mississippi, as the eastern boundary of...

Comparisons also need thought. A sentence such as: 'A was like B in having a sound knowledge of mathematics' may need a reference under A, but probably not under B. It is even less probable that: 'A, unlike B, had a sound knowledge of mathematics' would need an entry: 'B, no mathematician'.

Then there are names quoted as examples. If the names are merely mentioned, and other names might just as well have been chosen, they can be passed over. But if facts are related about them, consider including them. Lists of names, say of people present on a given occasion, or of species of plant found in a certain area, ought usually to be treated consistently; include all or none, unless there are good reasons for making a selection. Consistency of treatment should not be made into a fetish, but it is desirable, and becomes easier to achieve with practice.

2. TITLES; MARRIED WOMEN; PSEUDONYMS

Index references to a peer should be collected under either the title or the family name, with a cross-reference from the other:

> Kelvin, Lord (William Thomson)...
> Thomson, William, *see* Kelvin, Lord

When only three or four page numbers are involved, they may as well appear in both places, and instead of a cross-reference there should be a second entry:

> Thomson, William (Lord Kelvin)...

If the title is used for the main entry, then other peers should be treated similarly. In a book with many mentions of peers, consideration has to be given to the choice between name and title for the index. The family name is probably most useful in books for the specialist historian and genealogist, the title in books for the general reader, but the usage in the text must be taken into account. Different holders of the same title should be distinguished as 3rd Earl, 4th Earl, etc., and different commoners with the same surname by their forenames, and if necessary their professions.

'Sir' is usually added before the Christian names of knights, especially when, as with Raleigh, Sir Walter, and Sidney, Sir Philip, it is in accordance with general usage. But in a book on modern science, the best-known work of many of the scientific knights will be associated with their pre-knighthood period, and the usage of the text must be followed: Hopkins, F. G., and Thomson, J. J., may appropriately appear in the same form as Clerk-Maxwell, J., and Wilson, C. T. R., etc. Even Lord

Adrian and Lord Rutherford may appear as Adrian, E. D., and Rutherford, E., if references in the book are only to their earlier work under those names. Sir or other title is ignored in alphabetizing:

> Newton, Sir Isaac
> Newton, John

and

> Sidney, Algernon
> Sidney, Sir Philip
> Sidney, Robert, 1st Earl of Leicester

In a biography, the relatives of the hero, X, may have to be described as Mary Blank (aunt of X), Mary Blank (daughter of X), Mary Blank (sister of X); they can then be ranged by alphabetical order of relationship, or chronologically by date of birth. Individuals who have been known by successive titles may need cross-references for these as well as for family name or final title. A cardinal who became pope may be given a cross-reference from family name to papal name, or in the reverse direction if the book deals mainly with his activities as cardinal. The same applies to married women, who may be given a cross-reference from maiden name to married name, or in the reverse direction if the maiden name is better known. Pseudonyms also need cross-references, usually from pseudonym to real name, but in the reverse direction if the pseudonym is better known, as with George Eliot and Mark Twain.

3. SAINTS AND KINGS

A collection of kings, popes, saints, nobles, and emperors, all called by the same name, is sometimes indexed in hierarchic order, but though saints, followed by popes, are always put at the top, and commoners at the bottom, it is hard to fix the intermediate order of precedence, especially if the persons are from different countries. It is more satisfactory, and easier, to range the names in alphabetical order of titles:

> Nicholas, Antipope
> Nicholas, Czar of Russia
> Nicholas, Grand Duke of Russia
> Nicholas, King of Denmark
> Nicholas, Pope
> Nicholas, Saint

Though saints are indexed under their names, with the title saint to follow, saint comes first when the name is that of a place, such as St Andrews, St Quentin, or in such expressions as St John's wort, St Vitus's dance. The same ruling applies to names of people other than saints:

John Peel (song)	King William Street
Peel, John, huntsman	William IV

Even when written St, the word is alphabetized as saint. Foreign names in which St stands for San, Sankt, Santa, Santo, etc., are probably best dealt with by writing them out in full. French Sainte is abbreviated Ste, and follows St. There is no definite ruling about modern saints known by both Christian name and surname. Some indexers put:

Loyola, St Ignatius
Xavier, St Francis

Others prefer:

Francis Xavier, St
Ignatius Loyola, St

Modern female saints are known by their Christian names without surnames, and are indexed accordingly:

Bernadette of Lourdes, Ste
Thérèse of Lisieux, Ste

With many kings of the same name, those of each country are collected in numerical order, the countries following each other alphabetically. If descriptive epithets, such as 'the Great', 'the Pious', are included, they should be put in brackets after the king's number, to avoid breaking into the alphabetical sequence of countries; matter in brackets is usually *hors concours* with respect to alphabetization.

Whether to index the native or the English form of a foreign king's name must depend on the usage of the author, but the indexer would prefer the foreign form, because he can more easily arrange Heinrich/Henri/Henry than a mass of Henries.

A knotty point is the correct phrase to follow the name of the British monarch. 'Elizabeth I, Queen of England', or 'Elizabeth I of England', yes; but 'Elizabeth II, Queen of Great Britain and Northern Ireland and Her other Realms and Territories' is a little unwieldy. One way out of the difficulty is to put simply 'Elizabeth II', remembering that British postage stamps also do not specify their country of origin.

4. COMPOUND NAMES

The Scottish prefixes, Mac, Mc, and M', are all alphabetized as if they were spelt Mac. But note that Americans arrange these names as they are written. Irish names such as O'Flaherty and O'Toole are treated as single words; the apostrophe is ignored.

Foreign names beginning with De and Van that have become naturalized in Britain or the United States are indexed with the prefix in front, under D or V: De Morgan, De Quincey, Van Buren, Van Dyck. But French, German, Italian, Spanish and Portuguese names with prefixes meaning 'of' are indexed under the following word:

> Albuquerque, Affonso d'
> Annunzio, Gabriele d'
> Bismarck, Prince Otto von
> Cervantes, Miguel de
> Gaulle, General de
> Goethe, J. W. von
> Maupassant, Henri de
> Montmorency, Anne de

Dutch names beginning with Van (meaning 'of') or Van der (meaning 'of the') are also indexed under the following part of the name in Dutch books, but tend to appear in English indexes as Van Diemen, Van Rijn etc. This is perhaps because in some well-known names of this kind, the prefix and the rest have come to be joined: Vancouver, Vanderbilt, Vansittart. In Belgium, unlike Holland, names beginning with De and Van are indexed under the prefixes.

In Spanish names such as Goya y Lucientes, the y, meaning 'and' joins the father's and mother's surnames, and both should be given in the entry:

> Goya y Lucientes, F. J. de

The two names are often used without the conjunction, so that when three names are given for a Spaniard, it is likely that only the first is a forename.

Another prefix that is subordinated to the next part of the word in alphabetizing is al- at the beginning of Arabic names, though it is usually left in its place and not inverted:

> Fahrenheit, G. D.
> al-Farabi
> Faraday, Michael
> Fischer, Emil

Arabic names beginning with the prefix Ibn ('son of'), on the other hand, go under letter I. A full Arabic name may include personal name, father's and sometimes grandfather's name, and description of trade or place of origin: Omar ibn-Ibrahim al-Khayyam: Omar son of Ibrahim, the tent-maker. Choice of which part to index in any particular case must generally follow the usage in the text; if it refers consistently to Ibn Sīnā, the name should not be metamorphosed in the index into: Abū 'Ali al-Husam ibn 'Abdallah ibn Sīnā, though a cross-reference from Abū 'Ali might be wanted.

5. ORIENTAL NAMES

Chinese names have the family name placed first, so they are indexed without inversion:

> K'ung Fu-tze
> Mao Tse-tung
> Sun Yat-sen

The Japanese have adopted the Western system of forename followed by surname, so modern Japanese names must be inverted.

The indexing of names in an Oriental language requires a special study, the first thing to learn being to distinguish names from such titles as U and Daw in Burmese names, Pandit and Sri in Indian ones, Tenku and Tuanku in Malaysian ones, and Shaykh and Mawlay in Islamic ones. Use of surnames often differs between Westernized and other individuals, and in some countries is undergoing change.

MAKING THE INDEX: III

I. PAGE NUMBERS

Accuracy in transcribing page numbers is all-important, and difficult to ensure. The first essential is to form the habit of glancing back at the page number as soon as the entry has been written, to check that the number of the previous page is not still being recorded. Also important is especial care in writing numbers; it is usually obvious when a badly written word should be checked, but confusion between o and 6 may not be noticed. Revision of a long index gives an opportunity of checking many page numbers.

When several pages of the book deal continuously with one subject, a reference such as 63–72 is wanted. Scattered mentions on several pages are shown by separate figures: 63, 64, 67, 72; or by 63–72 *passim* ('here and there'), if the subject appears on practically every page. When a mention occurs at the bottom of a page, and continues to the next page, it helps in locating it to put 63–4, not simply 63. Some indexers uphold the ideal of indicating how many times a subject is mentioned on a single page: 63 *ter*, or 63^3, just as some think subdivided page numbers (63 a, 63 b, 63 c, 63 d) are necessary for large two-column pages in encyclopaedias, etc.

Note that it is not unknown for page numbers on the proofs to be misprinted. Corrections to the proofs may alter pagination, spelling of names, etc.; the author-indexer can deal with this, but the non-author indexer working on first proofs may not be informed of alterations; this accounts for some errors in indexes.

2. DATES AND OTHER FIGURES

It is important to keep the numbers representing page references separate from any other figures (except Roman numerals after the names of rulers, which need cause no confusion). Dates given to distinguish people and events should be placed in brackets, and so should the numbers sometimes wanted for the same key-word used more than once, to show the index-user that the first occurrence is not the only one:

> conductivity (1), electric
> conductivity (2), thermal

Brackets should also enclose references to the text in the *index locorum* of a book on a classical author:

> Horace: *Odes* I (2. 1), 34–7; (3. 6), 45–6, 67
> *Odes* II (5. 1), 45, 60–2

The numbers in brackets refer to poem and line. Another case for the use of brackets is in the combined author index and bibliography:

> Holmes, A., 1946, *Nature, Lond.*, **151**, 680–4. (352)

the last figure indicating the page where this article is referred to in the book being indexed.

Sometimes a number is best spelled out as a word:

> arithmetic
> in base twelve, 12, 16
> in base two, 12, 14–15

3. THE SUBJECT OF THE BOOK

How to deal in the index with the subject of the book is a disputed point, especially as regards biographies. There is said to have been a novice indexer once who gave the subject of the book a page reference from page 1 to the last page inclusive. Some indexers maintain that the subject of the book should have no index entry at all. Other (and more numerous) indexers construct an elaborate many-column entry, which in effect summarizes the whole book, and which, however well-designed, is often too long for easy reference. As G. V. Carey has written, this sort of entry is invaluable to the reviewer who wants to be saved the trouble of reading the book, but not helpful for ordinary readers. An intermediate party of indexers favours a compromise. When the book is a biography of *X*, his various activities are indexed under appropriate headings, such as:

> Barchester, *X*'s house at
> Bogota, *X* Minister at
> Eton, *X* at
> Foreign Office, *X* Under-Secretary at
> Madrid, *X* Ambassador at
> Matterhorn, *X*'s ascent of
> Oxford, *X* at
> Peace Conference, *X* attends
> *Recollections of an Ambassador*, by *X*

Teheran, *X* Chargé d'Affaires at
Washington, *X*'s visits to
etc.

Under *X*'s name in the index are placed only such personal matters as his birth, marriage, and death, his characteristics, hobbies, illnesses, and honours. A note describing the method used should perhaps be supplied at the head of the index, or the head of the entry for *X*.

4. LONG ENTRIES

Before too many page references accumulate on a card, sub-headings should be sketched out, and only references to general descriptions should be attached to the key-word. While recognizing that rearrangement may be necessary during revision, every effort should be made to collect like to like – and here a pre-reading of the book or chapter is a help.

A string of not more than five or six page numbers after a heading or sub-heading is permissible, but after that sub-division should be contrived if possible. There are exceptions, the chief one being in author indexes for scientific books, in which several lines of page references may follow the name of an author particularly prolific in papers, or particularly often quoted. The usual convention is to print in different type the page references to the author's papers in lists of references at the ends of articles or chapters, so that the long list of page numbers in ordinary type is at least punctuated by others in bold type or italics.

Sometimes it seems impossible to break down a string of page references, for they are all found to refer to the same statement, even if in different words. This may happen in a book with contributions by several authors, and also in a book by someone with 'a bee in his bonnet', or merely a habit of repeating himself.

5. DOUBLE ENTRY

The possible need for putting an index entry in two (or more) places must be kept in mind. A paragraph about gannets on Ailsa Craig probably needs references under both 'gannets' and 'Ailsa Craig', and one about trade union law under both 'law, trade union' and 'trade unions, law relating to'.

It is easy to forget one-half of the double-entry process, which leads to such absurdities as:

> Ailsa Craig, gannets on, 7, 29, 101
> gannets, on Ailsa Craig, 26, 29, 152

When they are printed next to one another, the inconsistency between the two entries is glaring, but it is not so apparent when they are pages apart. This fault is often found in imperfectly revised indexes.

6. SPLIT ENTRIES

Care must be taken not to have entries for two synonyms or near synonyms, both used in the text, with references split between the two when they should have been collected under one, with a cross-reference from the other. It is comparatively easy to deal with such pairs as freedom/liberty, press/newspapers, Athene/Minerva, Taiwan/Formosa, V1/flying bomb, taxonomy/classification, aspirin/acetylsalicylic acid. In the case of Russia/U.S.S.R., the terms may have been used loosely about the modern state, when one should be chosen as the heading with a cross-reference from the other, or they may refer to pre- and post-revolutionary times, when there should be two separate entries with *see also* references. It is more difficult to organize the references to such overlapping pairs of words as schools/education, food/nutrition, state/nation, and much thought may be required as to exact meanings. It may be necessary to have what appear at first sight to be superfluous entries, e.g.:

> slave trade
> slavery
> slaves

to cover the various aspects of a subject accurately.

Synonyms are particularly liable to be found in books containing contributions by several authors.

7. MINOR MENTIONS

According to the type of index, a passing mention of person or place may be safely ignored, or may require to be entered. Some indexes have to be all-inclusive, as for example in definitive editions of the letters of famous people. When all references to a name have been divided as far as possible into appropriate sub-headings, a residue of references may remain, only alike in being unimportant, and not associable with each other or any of the sub-headings so far devised. One of the following expressions can then act as a final sub-heading to introduce these residual references: 'also', 'other references', 'mentioned'. The last-named is employed in this way in the indexes to Churchill's *Second World War*.

8. INDEXING FROM GALLEY PROOFS

There is sometimes a requirement for indexing from galley proofs. This should not be undertaken unless really necessary; it has two drawbacks, first that it takes longer, because of the need for altering the galley-sheet numbers to page numbers, and secondly that the process of alteration, when the page proofs finally arrive, introduces an additional chance of error. If it has to be done, mark on the galley sheets the exact position of the beginning of each page of the page proofs, by drawing a line from the margin into the text, and writing the page number on the margin end of the line. Then take each card in turn, look up the references on the appropriate galley sheets, and enter the new numbers on the card in an ink of different colour from that originally used; it is as well to cross out the galley-sheet numbers at the same time.

REVISING THE CARDS

Having made all the entries on the cards, the novice is apt to think that the index is finished, except for typing and minor details. This may be true for a simple index. But a long complex one may not be much more than half done. Badly selected entries cannot be made into a good index by revision, but well-selected entries may give a poor index if not properly revised. Revision can often turn unsatisfactory indexes into useful ones.

The revision must be complete and methodical, each card being taken in turn.

(1) Consider whether the entry is really necessary. If it is too unimportant or too vague to be useful, now is the time to

discard it, but lay the card aside rather than tearing it up; entries of that particular kind may after all prove to be wanted.

(2) Ponder over the wording: is it appropriate, and as concise as possible? If there is a choice, use a noun rather than an adjective for beginning the entry. Here are a few examples from an actual index:

> facultative parasites
> obligate parasites
> preventive inoculation
> protective fungicides

The two first would be better as additional sub-headings to the existing entry for parasitism. Of two page numbers against the next, one is already found under inoculation, preventive, and the other should join it. Protective fungicides should become an additional sub-heading under fungicides.

But in other entries in the same index, opening adjectives are acceptable:

> Contagious Diseases (Animals) Act
> spontaneous generation
> wetting agents

Prefer the more specific and concrete to the more general and abstract term. To quote again, not:

> Decline of agriculture in Great Britain

but:

> Agriculture, decline of

(3) If the same subject also appears in another entry, check that both have the same page numbers (cf. double entry, pp. 25–6). Look out for near-synonyms and split entries (see p. 26).

(4) Is it necessary to add *see also* at the end of the entry to direct the reader to further information? Ought a cross-reference to be made to this entry from another, or ought this entry to be converted into a cross-reference? If the entry is, or becomes, a cross-reference, check that the entry it refers to really exists; do not send the reader on what G. V. Carey has called a wild-goose chase.

(5) When possible, avoid having entries under both singular

and plural forms of a noun. The plural tends to be the preferable form. E.g. not:

author, as indexer
authors, books by several

but:

authors
books by several
as indexers

Occasionally it is convenient to use the either/or form, e.g. muscle(s), industry(ies). Very occasionally, both forms *are* required:

wood, microscopic structure of
woods, plant and animal life in

(6) When several consecutive entries begin with the same word, it is usually preferable to repeat it, rather than to leave a space, or to use a rule, to represent it. The following entry from an actual index shows an awkward arrangement:

National Chemical Laboratory
economy
income
Physical Laboratory
Research Council

which is much improved if written out in full:

National Chemical Laboratory
national economy
national income
National Physical Laboratory
National Research Council

Even with successive members of a family, it avoids confusion to repeat the surname for each one.

(7) An entry that fills one card altogether, or spreads over several cards, needs special attention. Almost certainly the sub-headings will have to be rearranged, improved, rephrased, and made more compact; most references should be looked up, to see if the material is properly classified, or whether additional or alternative sub-headings should be devised. A long sub-heading may duplicate one under another heading, and it may be advisable to cancel one of the pair, and replace it by a cross-reference. If it is decided to keep both, check that the page

numbers agree. It is usually best to rewrite the whole entry on a fresh card, and it is pleasing to find that what was spread over several cards can often be organized neatly on one. Keep the old cards, in case some doubt arises about page numbers or omissions.

(8) When there are several 'parallel' long entries, say for several countries or counties, or for successive kings or prime ministers, try to make all the entries of a set similar in organization. It helps the index-user if he finds a pattern underlying the index.

(9) Now is the time to deal with names mentioned by the author without any forenames or initials. A bald surname in the index looks to an indexer's eye disagreeably unfinished, and a confession of failure, and if possible he should provide a name or initials to complete it, with the aid of his works of reference. It may be extremely difficult to do so. Authors mentioned in scientific books may have to be pursued to the original papers for their initials – sometimes only to find, in French and German journals, that the characters are described simply as M. (for Monsieur) Quelqu'un, and H. (for Herr) Jemand. Resort to the original paper may also be required when a single author is mentioned both as A. B. Somebody and B. A. Somebody. Indexers who have not access to adequate libraries can only draw the attention of the author or publisher to lack or discrepancy of initials.

In the last resort, one can fall back on qualifying the unadorned surname by Dr or Mr, or a word or two of description:

> Brown (gardener at *Y* Castle)
> Jones (*X*'s fellow-prisoner)
> Robinson (traveller in Tartary)

(10) Attention should also be given to blanks left for dates, etc., in the stress of selecting the entries, and to adjusting the sub-headings to suit the lay-out that is to be adopted. Nothing should be left unsettled to interrupt the process of typing, or to invite alterations of the typescript.

RE-READING

When making a complex index to a long book, some re-reading of the book is desirable after revising the cards. During the progression through the book, the indexer's viewpoint has probably altered somewhat, affecting the choice of entries, and during the process of revision the pattern of the index has gradually become defined, making clearer what ought to be included. A rapid re-reading of the early chapters usually provides a number of additional entries for matters only now seen to be important, and also additional references for existing entries, perhaps not originally opened until some way on in the book. Re-reading should be continued until it is found that no further additions and alterations are being made, usually about half to two-thirds of the way through the book. A final re-reading is probably of more value in producing a good index than a pre-reading of the whole book, though the latter should by no means be omitted if time allows. Experience enables an indexer to decide whether re-reading is necessary.

THE INDEXER AS PROOF-READER

In the course of indexing a book, the non-author indexer may notice points that seem to need correction, and he can contribute usefully to the production by calling the attention of the author or publisher to them. He is usually working on un-corrected proofs, so that many of the points will be discovered by others, but proof-reading is very much a case of two heads being better than one.

Sometimes it is necessary to seek a ruling as to preferred spelling for names given in two forms, either of which may be acceptable, but both of which in one index are not. The discrepancy may be due to differences in transliteration of a name from a language with a different alphabet from ours, or one form may be a mis-spelling. Dates, also, are liable to be given differently on different pages, especially in a book by several authors.

The careful reading necessary for indexing may disclose grammatical errors, such as lack of agreement between the subject and verb of a sentence. It may be found that columns of figures lack headings, or that the numbers of two text figures have been interchanged. Names for units are sometimes lacking from graphs and other scientific figures. Some of these are matters that the indexer is more likely to notice than other proof-readers are. Occasionally an author makes a statement that the indexer knows with certainty to be wrong, particularly if the author strays a little aside from his own field of knowledge, and enters what happens to be the indexer's own speciality. Here it is helpful to send a note of explanation, perhaps quoting some reference book.

There is of course the reverse case: the author can correct mistakes made by the indexer through ignorance or carelessness, and should have (and take) the opportunity of reading the index typescript before it goes to the printer.

TYPING AND TYPOGRAPHY

Though printers can sometimes be persuaded to accept legibly handwritten indexes on numbered cards, they charge less for setting from typescript, and though the process of typing is an opportunity for errors to creep in, it is also a chance for a final polish, and allows the indexer to show his typographical intentions clearly. Typescript should be double-spaced, including sub-headings.

Typing is a particularly important stage in making an index to a specified length. The lines must be made with the same number of characters as they are to have in the printed index, to enable the length to be judged accurately. A final pruning is quickly achieved on the typescript, even if this means some degree of defacement.

The commonest errors in typing are mistakes in page numbers, and omission of entries owing to cards sticking together, against both of which the indexer should be continually on his guard. It is also easy to forget the space that should be left after the entries for each successive letter of the alphabet. A safeguard is to separate the cards for one letter, check them through for correct alphabetical order, and complete the typing of this batch before returning it to the box; then it is natural to leave a space before starting on the next batch.

It was formerly the custom to start each entry with a capital letter, but using lowercase letters to begin entries other than those for proper names gives some slight help to the searching eye, and is now more usual.

The matter of lay-out for the index was considered earlier (see pp. 8–10). Note on those pages that run-on sub-headings need only one indentation at the left-hand margin, whereas set out sub-headings require two or three.

The usual mode of punctuation at the present time is to put a comma after the key-word if it is followed by page references, but a colon if directly followed by run-on sub-headings; the latter are separated by semicolons. No mark of punctuation is put at the end of a row of page numbers not followed by a further word. There is a slight movement towards minimizing punctuation by omitting the comma after the key-word.

If figures in bold type are wanted, they should be underlined with a handwritten wavy line. In a long author index with bold figures (for references to lists of papers) scattered through the page numbers, it saves much time if the handwritten wavy line for these is replaced by typed underlining; one instruction to the printer can cover this substitution, and can be acceptable with adequate explanation.

Typewritten underlining usually indicates italics. Note that in botanical and zoological works, the names of species are given in italics: *Bellis perennis*, *Homo sapiens*; but the names of orders, families, etc., are not; Compositae, Crustacea, Insectivora. Names of books and ships are usually italicized.

Two copies at least of the index should be made so that author and printer can each have one. Three copies are sometimes asked for.

CORRECTING THE PROOFS OF THE INDEX

To correct the proofs of one's index is an important part of the task, though an opportunity of doing so is not always offered, and time does not always allow of it. The indexer is more likely than other readers to notice misprints in his work, and has a clearer mental picture of the design of the index. He does well to mention to the publisher his willingness to read the proof, and to do so in a minimum of time, for when the index is in proof, the moment for going to press is in all probability approaching rapidly. If the indexer has not kept a copy of the index, he should ask for one with the proof, but it is possible, and indeed in some ways desirable, to correct the proofs from the index cards, which should always be kept until this stage is over.

The printer may send two copies of the proof, one (marked 'return this copy') bearing the corrections of the printer's reader. The indexer should write on the other copy at first, to allow for change of mind, and transfer the final version of his instructions to the marked copy. The author or subeditor may have made alterations to the index before it was printed; these must be respected, but should be checked to see if they observe the indexer's conventions as to order of sub-headings, etc., and queried if out of step. It is usual to mark printer's errors in red, and alterations desired by the other parties in another colour, for purposes of calculating costs. It is imperative to make necessary corrections only, since they are expensive luxuries at this stage.

The conventions of proof-correcting are described in works of reference, and should be carefully observed. Mistakes to look out for are those that involve the ranging of the left-hand edge of the column – sub-headings appearing as main headings and vice versa – and errors in punctuation. A line is sometimes omitted, or printed twice.

CONCLUSION

A last aspect of indexing may be mentioned. Each index presents a new problem, and requires new devices to obtain the best results. Consequently the indexer is always learning, not only from the books he indexes, but also about indexing itself. Consequently also, he is always dissatisfied with his earlier productions.

INDEX (about 8%)